FABRIC FLOWERS FOR BEGINNER

Complete Step by steps guide on fabric flowers, effective methods, tips, techniques and procedures on how to make fabrics flowers for beginner

Table of Contents

CHAPTER ONE 3

    INTRODUCTION 3

    STEP BY STEP INSTRUCTIONS TO UTILIZE YOUR TEXTURE BLOSSOMS 6

    THE MOST EFFECTIVE METHOD TO MAKE TEXTURE BLOSSOMS 8

    THE MOST EFFECTIVE METHOD TO BEGIN SOME BLOSSOM MAKING TIPS 12

CHAPTER TWO 15

    PETAL BLOSSOM 15

    MAKE GLADIOLUS BLOSSOM 18

    MAKE A STRAIGHT FORWARD COLLAPSED BLOOM 20

    MAKE GLOBE AMARANTH BLOSSOM 21

CHAPTER THREE 24

    STEP BY STEP INSTRUCTIONS TO MAKE A TEXTURE ROSE 24

    INSTRUCTIONS TO SEW A GLOSSY SILK TEXTURE BLOSSOM 25

CHAPTER FOUR 30

    DO-IT-YOURSELF TEXTURE ROSE CHOICES 30

THE END 38

CHAPTER ONE

INTRODUCTION

Thinking about how to make texture blossoms? There are many plans around, and everything relies on the look you need to accomplish. I for one love this basic plan, which is really simple to make thus adaptable. Ideal for sprucing up a plain outfit, changing over into a clasp, or make one to join to a hairpin. These lovely blossoms are a flexible princess gift thought.

Materials for this venture, you will require:

1. Beautiful texture

2. Glass or round layout

3. Cardboard (simply scrounge through your reusing container to discover some)

4. Designer's chalk or a pencil, we might procure a commission for buys utilizing our connections, as portrayed in our partner exposure.

5. Scissors

6. Needle and string pick a string to match your texture. I have utilized dark here to make sure you can see my fastens without any problem.

7. A pin backing, self locking pin, or plain clasp.

Directions

You'll, right off the bat, need to make a circle layout to use for removing your texture. Follow around a little glass onto cardboard, and cut out the cardboard circle. Utilizing your cardboard layout, follow 14 circles onto your texture and cut these out. Here I am utilizing a wonderful crude silk remainder I found in the deal container at my neighborhood texture store. It has normal firmness and is ideally suited for making ravishing blossoms with. Put two circles of texture on top of each other and secure along with a straightforward fasten. This will be the foundation of your bloom. Take four circles of texture for the subsequent stage. Overlap each into equal parts, and secure with a little join to the focal point of your base. With the excess eight texture circles, overlay each into quarters and secure for certain join at the base. Sew four quarters into the focal point of your base. Presently fasten the last four quarters into the middle and tie off under. Cushion up your "petals" and you're finished.

STEP BY STEP INSTRUCTIONS TO UTILIZE YOUR TEXTURE BLOSSOMS

Since you have made a wonderful blossom you'll need to show it off. Why not sew or stick your blossom onto a plain top to dress it up a little, or connect your bloom to a pin and pop it in your hair. Simply sew or heated glue it onto your pin base and you're finished. The guidelines above cover the fundamental bloom plan. In any case, in the event that you need to you can add more texture circles for a more full look, or add a couple of layers of tulle for extra glitz. You could likewise utilize pinking shears to remove your texture circles on the off chance that you need a more finished look. Considering how to make texture blossoms? There are many plans around, and everything relies on the look you need to accomplish. I for one love this straightforward plan, which is really simple to make thus adaptable. Ideal for sprucing up a plain outfit, changing over into a clasp, or make one to join to a fastener. These lovely blossoms are a flexible princess gift thought.

THE MOST EFFECTIVE METHOD TO MAKE TEXTURE BLOSSOMS

Materials

For this undertaking, you will require:

1. Beautiful texture

2. Glass or round layout

3. Cardboard simply scavenge through your reusing receptacle to discover some.

4. Designer's chalk or a pencil

We might procure a commission for buys utilizing our connections, as depicted in our member revelation.

1. Scissors

2. Needle and string pick a string to match your texture. I have utilized dark here to make sure you can see my fastens without any problem.

3. A pin backing, self locking pin, or plain fastener.

Directions

Right off the bat you'll have to make a circle layout to use for removing your texture. Follow around a little glass onto cardboard, and cut out the cardboard circle. Here I am utilizing a lovely crude silk leftover I found in the deal canister at my neighborhood texture store. It has regular firmness and is ideal for making ravishing blossoms with. Put two circles of texture on top of each other and secure along with a basic fasten. This will be the foundation of your blossom. Take four circles of texture for the following stage. Crease each down the middle, and secure with a little join to the focal point of your base. With the excess eight texture circles, crease each into quarters and secure for certain lines at the base. Sew four quarters into the focal point of your base. Presently line the last four quarters into the middle and tie off under. Cushion up your "petals" and you're finished.

Since you have made a wonderful blossom you'll need to show it off. Why not sew or stick your bloom onto a plain top to dress it up a little, or join your blossom to a fastener and pop it in your hair? Simply sew or craft glue it onto your hairpin base and you're finished. The directions above cover the essential blossom plan. However, on the off chance that you need to you can add more texture circles for a more full look, or add a couple of layers of tulle for extra glitz. You could likewise utilize pinking shears to remove your texture circles on the off chance that you need a more finished look. I'm one-sided about blossoms. Who isn't? They are wonderful. When made with texture, they can be utilized to change basic looking pieces of clothing and accomplices to remarkable ones of excellence. When I began making them I got the hang of something important to me. It is just exhausting things like cooking that I abhorrence to do. I can make these handcrafted blossoms day in and day out.

THE MOST EFFECTIVE METHOD TO BEGIN SOME BLOSSOM MAKING TIPS

A few primer focuses I learned while making hand tailored texture blossoms

1. The most compelling things you should make the blossoms are the texture for blossoms, sharp scissors, slight needle, matching string, wire, green tape for

covering tail, gum, old scissors to cut wire, cotton for stuffing if necessary, stamens to keep in the focal point of the blossoms likewise called pips you really want to purchase these.

2. You can utilize texture pieces of organdy, silk, fake silk, voile, velvet, chiffon and even yarns to make these blossoms.

3. The stems/stalks of blossoms, which are made of wire can be covered with green tape with cement on it, inclination pieces of green silk, velvet or green organdy, white or shaded weaving cotton or silk.

4. Cut every one of the petals before you begin gathering the bloom.

5. On the off chance that you are making blossoms with firm petals the texture ought to be solidified you can harden the bloom making texture by dunking it in an answer of gum and water press before totally dry.

CHAPTER TWO

PETAL BLOSSOM

Instructions to make the petal texture bloom.

1. Cut a texture piece of 6 inches wide and 12.5 inches long

2. Overlap it considerably

3. Measure 2.5 crawls from one finish of the strip so you structure 5 segments.

4. Mark this on the collapsed texture. 1 second of 31 seconds Volume 0%.

5. Make running lines as in the image above along these imprints.

Presently assemble the texture by pulling the string from the two sides.

THE FIVE PETAL BLOSSOM AND FINISH THIS BLOOM WITH A BUTTON IN THE MIDDLE

1. Make Morning magnificence blossoms

Morning wonders are delightful trumpet-formed blossoms in pink, purple-blue, maroon, or white. It is a wildflower you see developing all over the place. My morning brilliance bloom doesn't look as sublime as the genuine one yet now that you will know how to make it, perhaps you can develop it.

2. Remove organdy texture 2 - 3 inches wide by 5 inches long.

Make whip lines or use sewing foot to stitch the edge with a differentiating string or utilize the lighter to consume the edges of the texture as I did. You simply need a decent lip along the petal edge.

3. Join the short edges of this texture with a French crease; you will get a cylinder like this. Look at the post on French crease if don't have the foggiest idea how to make it.

4. Make a circle with the wire. Insert a few pips inside the circle.

5. Keep wire with the pips in the texture cylinder and afterward assemble the

center of the cylinder and bind with string. This will frame the petal of your blossom. Presently accumulate the rose base the same way.

MAKE GLADIOLUS BLOSSOM

To make gladiola blossoms you really want slight and fresh texture, organdy and voile are great for this. You likewise need a few stamens pips and of course botanical wire and green tape and matching string for integrating the petals. Remove 3 inch square texture pieces. For a little bloom you really want 3 petals.

6 PETALS REQUIRE FOR MAKING GREATER BLOSSOMS

A depiction of how the crease of the gladiolus petal is finished overlay the texture piece slantingly by the middle, so the contrary corners meet. Presently carry the left and right corners to the base corner. Presently rehash this equivalent overlay, carrying the corner to the base corner. Wind the sides a little to the back and bind the petal at the base with matching string. You can make gladioli spikes by orchestrating these blossoms and a bud or more bud is made with one single petal made the same way along a long firm wire. As you add the blossoms you have made cover the focal wire with grebe tape. The buds come at the top, then three petal blossoms and afterward six petal blossoms. You can add in the middle between.

MAKE A STRAIGHT FORWARD COLLAPSED BLOOM

Assuming you have some 3-inch squares left over from creating gladiola you can make this bloom. It is a straightforward construction. A fail to remember me not blossom can be made this way with blue petals. Crease the square slantingly and afterward assemble the sides to the center base corner. Tie at the base. Make four or five petals and add a few pips in the center or another petal made the same way in an alternate variety fabric. Integrate all that with wire in the center to finish one bloom.

MAKE GLOBE AMARANTH BLOSSOM

The globe amaranth is the blossom that never blurs something to do with the way that it has no water in its petals, I think. I generally believed that this blossom is just in violet or maroon however appears as though they are accessible in pink, white and so on and they are heavenly. To make these blossoms, you want fleece yarn and an old scale alongside some wire. Simply wrap the fleece yarn on the scale one finish of the scale a few 40-45 times. Make a stunning texture rose to add to your home stylistic layout or to give Mother for mother's day. A ravishing high quality gift clincher you can sew manually or machine. Staggering home enhancement. Blossoms are perfect for improvement of your home feasting table, weddings, workplaces, and essentially some other sort of room. The issue with genuine blossoms is that they should be dealt with appropriately or they in the long run shrink. Also, when I'm not home, nobody makes sure to water them consistently, regardless of how frequently I remind them. However, because of my sort spouse being a piece languid, I thought of an option in contrast to genuine blossoms.

CHAPTER THREE

TEXTURE ROSES

They look awesome. They are likewise extremely simple and enjoyable to make. You can make a couple of them in less than 60 minutes. Simply adhere to the directions from this instructional exercise and you'll complete in practically no time. We incidentally in connection to merchandise presented by sellers to assist the peruse with tracking down significant items. A portion of the connections might be partner meaning we procure a little commission on the off chance that a thing is bought.

STEP BY STEP INSTRUCTIONS TO MAKE A TEXTURE ROSE

Supplies and devices

1. Texture - 3" x 40-50" long segment of glossy silk and you can likewise utilize silk or chiffon.

2. Matching string

3. Scissors or rotating shaper and a cutting mat

4. Ruler or estimating tape

5. Sewing machine a straight forward machine will really do fine and dandy, or you might hand sew this, albeit as a matter

of fact it will require you greater investment.

Notes: You can utilize various materials glossy silk, silk and even chiffon. Follow me with the expectation of complimentary examples and instructional exercises.

INSTRUCTIONS TO SEW A GLOSSY SILK TEXTURE BLOSSOM

If it's not too much trouble, appreciate and remember to like and buy to be stayed up with the latest with new recordings really.

Directions:

Stage 1: Measure and cut the texture strip. You should cut the glossy silk/chiffon into a really lengthy piece. It ought to be 40 to 50 inches long, and around 3 - 3.5 inches wide. Cut longer portion of texture on the off chance that you need more voluminous rose. The more extended your piece of texture, the greater your rose will be.

Stage 2: Overlay the upper right corner down. Take one corner of the texture piece, pull it down, and overlay the texture so it contacts the inverse long edge, around two crawls from the top. You will wind up with a little, sporadic triangle toward one side of the whole texture piece.

Stage 3: Make a slanting cut. Presently cut the texture somewhat slantingly where the side of the overlay contacts the long edge. The corner you pulled down before. Cut towards the nearer end of the texture.

Stage 4: Begin sewing. Presently fasten along the briefest edge of the triangle. Whenever you have done that, crease the texture so the long edges meet and make a couple of join. Continue collapsing and sewing the whole way to the furthest limit of the strip.

Stage 5: Accumulate the portion of silk. Pull the finish of the string to accumulate the texture strip.

Stage 6: Structure the focal point of the rose. Pull the start of the string significantly more to accumulate the focal point of the rose. Then change the get-together towards the middle.

Stage 7: See your blossom. Roll up your blossom and cushion it to perceive how you like it.

Stage 8: Unroll and begin sewing. Unroll the texture bloom and make a couple of join at the back to hold the middle. Continue rolling and sewing. At the point when you arrive at the finish of the strip make a protected bunch and trim the closures of the string.

Stage 9: Discretionary add a texture circle to the back. Cut a circle of texture and either stick it or join it to the rear of the blossom.

Stage 10: Discretionary add dot to the middle. Sew three medium white dots to the focal point of the bloom. That is all; your texture raised it prepared.

CHAPTER FOUR

DO-IT-YOURSELF TEXTURE ROSE CHOICES

1. Add stem to make a bouquet - Utilize a botanical wire to make a stem. Utilizing a spot of paste connect the rose to the stem.

2. Add Dots to the focal point of your rose for a more cleaned look.

3. Attach a felt or wool circle to the rear of the rose and use it as a table top design.

4. Turn it into a gift box clincher - utilize a touch of clear tape or vent to join it to a gift box for a genuinely noteworthy gift.

5. In all honesty, this really connects with food, so stay with me here. Two or three

weeks prior I showed you a look of my Christmas brightening and I had a few solicitations for an instructional exercise on the wreath I made. I've made bunches of texture roses previously, yet I hadn't remembered to put them on a wreath until I saw this one of every one of my email bulletins from Living Locarno. I had charming Christmas texture lying around in light of the fact that I like to purchase these pre-sliced quarters to use on top of containers like Peppermint Fudge Cupcake Containers, or Pie in a Container, or buttermilk syrup, hot fudge sauce, and sugar clean as presents.

6. So this was an ideal use for the left over. This is a speedy the way to on the

blossoms and afterward I'll show you how you can utilize them.

7. The shade of the texture is a higher priority than the real example on it. When the blossoms are moved you don't for even a moment see the example, simply the tones.

8. First you really want to cut a portion of texture about an inch to an inch and a half wide. The length decides the last width of the blossom. A 24" strip makes a blossom around 1" wide. In the event that you don't have an extremely lengthy piece of texture, which is OK, you can utilize more than one short strip on a solitary blossom, I'll make sense of in a moment.

9. Fold your strip in half so the right side is outwardly and it's long and thin. Place some texture stick around 2" down like these utilize one of a kind Join or Fluid Fasten stick.

10. Now simply roll it straight up. This will be the focal point of the blossom. I roll it around 7 or multiple times, simply eyeball it.

11. Keep your paste nearby. Hold the middle with one hand and with the other beginning contorting your texture around the middle, putting a spot of paste from time to time to maintain a reasonable level of control. You can bend the texture as little or however much you like, simply mess with it and you'll understand.

12. Then simply continue onward around and around. The cut edges will uncover little strings which add to the appeal.

13. When you get to the end simply stick the finish of your texture to the posterior of the blossom. Also, assuming you need the bloom bigger. Make another strip and paste the beginning finish to the rear of the blossom and forge ahead as you were. This one underneath utilized 2 pieces of 22" texture on.

14. When you're totally done you can do anything you desire with them. I just utilized create paste to stick them to a modest grape plant wreath, alongside certain berries and a little birdie, might you at any point spy him.

15. But there are heaps of purposes for these adorable seemingly insignificant details. For instance, get a few pins or clasps from the art store and paste them on the back utilizing a piece of felt. I was unable to see as my felt so I'm simply utilizing a clasp I as of now have made to show what I mean.

15. Sometimes you end up with a "stem" of sorts. On the off chance that you want a compliment blossom, simply trip it off with decent sets of scissors. Different times a stem like that is useful, similar to while sticking to my wreath.

16. Anyway, when your blossoms are done you can do loads of fun things with them.

17. Like bundle up Christmas treats, I let you know this had something to do with food and clasp or pin one or a few on the bundles. They're not difficult to join to the lace, or additionally the genuine gift tag.

18. They look absolutely charming, however at that point your gifts will be eager to such an extent that they can pull them off and utilize them. They look very charming stuck onto a cap.

19. on a sack or handbag or lapel. I referenced in my other post that these are an extraordinary television project. It's simply bustling work rolling and sticking, rolling and sticking, rolling and sticking, so pop in a decent film and you'll be shocked

at the number of you have done toward the end.

THE END

Printed in Great Britain
by Amazon